THE FIRE LIT
& NEARING

THE FIRE LIT
& NEARING

::: J.G. MCCLURE :::

INDOLENT BOOKS

Cover design: adam b. bohannon
Book design: Nieves Guerra
Book editor: Journey McAndrews

Published by Indolent Books,
an imprint of Indolent Arts Foundation, Inc.

www.indolentbooks.com
Brooklyn, New York
ISBN: 978-1-945023-09-5

It's something of a squeaky song.
Happy little mice, I think, eating through a sack of bones.
—Thomas Lux

CONTENTS

The Odyssey II

After the joy there are questions
why he alone returned, the trial

for his slaughter of servants and suitors
who after 20 years were the basis

of the island's economy: with their deaths
the butchers and bakers go hungry &

glare at the unshaven king, who strides
the streets nightly wailing *Ithaca Ithaca,*

waking the children & frightening the hounds.
He thinks of visiting the cyclops, of writing

the sorceress. He thinks the gods kept him
lost for pity, pity for the little man

who now tosses in his creaking bed
& dreams his little dreams of sailing

back to the horse's dark belly,
to huddled swordsmen & the smell of pitch,

the blind prophet not yet weeping,
the torches not yet touching

the great city not yet burned.
And what is Penelope beside The Idea

of Penelope, for whom he longs
beside the sea, watching the rise

and dip of distant masts? O gods,
may we find a way to her.

I

Multiverse Theory

There are worlds as real as this one for every way we never meet:
worlds where you get hit by a bus instead, or I do,
worlds where you are the one
driving the bus and the squishy
whistling noise I make as
I'm sucked under the wheels haunts you
so that you never drive a bus again, you become
a lobbyist against unsafe busing practices,
you symbolically bury the fenders of retired buses
in tasteful but under-attended twilight ceremonies you imagine
the man you hit with the bus would really have liked.
And there are others in which you find a way
not to think about any of that,
and instead keep driving the same bus for years, many years.

There are worlds where the two of us are both on the bus,
where we take the same bus route every day
and never speak, and there is nothing
especially tragic in this, because you
are just a stranger on a bus
like any of the other strangers
on any of the other buses I've ridden in my life—strangers

I must in some other worlds love deeply
and with whom I must have variable numbers of children
who will one day grow up to become bus drivers
because of the charming story of how their parents met
on a bus just like the bus that in some of those worlds
I must be riding home in, sitting beside you (stranger) right now.

There are of course worlds in which buses were never invented,
in which humans were never invented and little

eyeless monsters worm through primordial ooze
eating one another or not eating one another,
and their dull proto-fear is the closest thing to suffering
in worlds where attachment
has never been imagined
or missed.

I don't know if such worlds are better off than ours.
But there must be a world in which I do.

Café Terrace at Night

After you left, everything was sexual. Our old friend
blowing over the mug before she sipped,

how she tightened her hold as
we argued how to make our poems hurt.

Around us, the dogwoods were no help:
loosened buds and the air thick with pollen. I know

this was only transference, that even as she slipped
the ring down and up her finger

she wasn't really who I wanted (but
she was and was and was): we pour

our hungers over trees, friends, anything
manageably outside. In Van Gogh's painting,

see how the awning shields the drinkers
in their separate communions,

how the terrace suspends them
between cobblestones and starry

smudges illuminating
nothing, how the windows

of homes glow warm and bronze and
out-of-reach as I look

not to you, or her,
but to the canvas:

where branches push into view,
where seats shine out their emptiness,

where someone and her shadow
are leaving arm-in-arm.

The Cat

First she'd bring a mouse, a bird. Fur or feathers matted, eyes bulging, fang holes in the neck. Then one day a deer. The whole stag matted, bulging, fang-holed—she purred her tiny purrs. "Good cat," we said. "Nice kitty."

For a long time it was quiet. Then an SUV, wheels up and oil pooling. The tires twitched pitifully. She circled, rubbed, moved from leg to leg.

"We've got to tell someone."

"It only means she loves us."

We'd buried the car when she brought down the jet. Dazed passengers filed out one by one; they called us terrible names. We scratched behind her ears—what else could we do—as she batted the oxygen masks. When the army came with their tanks she ate their tanks and slinked toward the city. We heard great cries then silence.

Now she's dragging down the sun for us. The air gets hotter every day. Eggs boil inside their shells; pigeons burn mid-flight—but she looks so happy coming near, fire shimmering in her eyes.

Weeping, doomed, we lay out her favorite treats. In the end, there's only love.

Romantic

The 19th Century showed up drunk again;
Keats is sobbing on my couch something

about a nightingale. Wordsworth watches,
a disappointed dad sipping gin.

O Ellie, it should have been our time—
we were so good at sadness.

In the graveyard we kissed without irony
and you understood the spiritus mundi

is made of absinthe and frustration.
My doctor tells me I have no faith

in other humans, but I don't believe him
because he smokes no pipe. Don't you think

you could've found a way
to live with me? Had we just been

born 200 years ago, together
we could vomit laudanum, gently

holding back each other's hair.

Reverse

The man walks backward into a lamplit studio where
like him the woman is crying. They scream

in each other's faces until the tears recede
back into their eyes, turning them from red to white.

The two hold each other, grateful for this cure.

They undress and lie beneath a cool sheet,
make love and dress again. Months pass.

Their faces begin to soften, and the pair looks younger.
They take long, backward walks together.

Happy at last, each no longer needs the other.
They call, but spend most nights alone.

In the final scene, the two are sitting close at a bar.

He reaches into his coat and unfolds a paper
where her number is written. She clicks a pen and carefully

unwrites each digit. All nervous smiles,
the man moves to a different table.

He spits whiskey into a glass,
where cubes of ice are slowly forming.

Nothing Will Be Alright,
But Thank You Anyway

Want wants what it wants: in Magritte's *Les Amants,*
two lovers—their separate heads in sackcloth shrouds—
press together the spaces where their lips would be.

Under the sacks they can't have air enough,
wrapped in darkness and their own stale breathing,
but we want so much to believe they're happy

despite it all: though they'll never truly touch
or see past the tips of their own noses,
though at the wedding she'll remove her bridal veil

only to reveal the familiar veil, though they'll get a house
and raise children whose lives they'll infer
from muffled sounds, children who will

cry and teethe and grow old from
behind their own thick shrouds—
maybe still they're happy. Or at least

maybe they could be; we can't know after all
they *aren't* content: maybe never knowing
how your lover looks at you

is mercy, and they'll never have to pay
for sunglasses. The sacks might smell
richly of sandalwood and cinnamon.

Self Portrait as Man and Pet

You teach your Sadness tricks: *Speak*
you say, *Speak* and Sadness unhinges

his whiskery jaw, lets loose concertos
and ballads and arduous chapters

of the great Russian novels. *Good boy*
you say, *Play dead.* Sadness tries—

he really tries—but he wiggles
with pride, springs up to bound

around the house shedding ashes and
bottle caps everywhere. Sadness eats his kibbles

but he wants your burger too; he begs at first
then swallows the stove. He's guilty

for that and for pissing on the carpet
so he gives you dumb, soggy kisses

but takes to eating neighbors' cats.
He takes to eating neighbors. *No,* you say, *Bad,*

and Sadness hangs his massive head, drops
his tail to whine. It's too late. You rent a truck

and drive to the next county, lead him to the woods
and leave him there snuffling the underbrush.

But back home you find him in the yard,
charging you, heavy tongue flapping

backward in the wind. He is
a faithful Sadness. He loves you so much.

The Transience of All Things Walks into a Bar

or rather, a series of almost-but-
not-truly-identical bars flickering

one to the next so quick there's the illusion,
like a film reel, of a stable image: here,

a bartending hipster, Josh—whose thoughts
and cells are being replaced so imperceptibly

and inexorably that he is not really Josh but
a flickering of Joshes who pour a flickering of beers,

one of which The Transience of All Things nurses for years
between tequilas, more years and hoppy belches

until the pint is gone. By then the bar
is abandoned. In the rusting ruin

of the men's room, The Transience
of All Things misses what once was

the urinal. His favorite boot is wet; the leather
is probably ruined. For his part, Josh died

decades ago and there followed the usual
service: solemn preachers preaching,

solemnly, of Josh's many virtues, most of which
were vague but enough to bring comfort

to his children who were sure
they would never get past his death

but gradually did somehow until waking
one morning they didn't think of how

their father would never wake again;
this was the exact moment that defined

their emotional midlives but it went
unnoticed until much later when

it could be inferred but not remembered,
much to the distress of the children

who sensed it was exactly the sort of thing
they should be able to remember dammit.

On Recovery

Everyone in my family has to fight the bear.
The bear is old, older than my grandfather's

grandfather & his teeth are long
& yellow. I know his stratagems.

Say I'm at the airport: the bald man
at the bar with the blazer & briefcase

could be the bear: he could tear
out my eyeballs & the last thing they'd see

is my blood on the business bear's coat.
So I'm careful. I plan every egress;

I check beneath my car. I rarely sleep
& when I sleep I sleep with bear mace

under the pillow. So far the pillow
is not the bear. And you my dear—

I believe you're not the bear.
Those lips I love are not ursine & you

never roar plucking salmon from a stream.
Thank you, for staying despite him.

Go on—sleep and I'll keep vigil:
all night the willow will rasp

our window. Far below will be homes,
fields, all the wide earth rustling

with the gentle snuffling of the bear.

The Astronaut

It turns out there's nothing to think of but yourself.
There are stars, yes, and Earth,
hanging there like a big wet baseball.
It's nice at first. Then it's routine, then it's new
versions of the old problems. Insomnia,
for instance. You spend a life
sticking your head on a pillow, but now the pillow
just floats away. So you tape it to your face.
Every night you tape the pillow to the side of your face
and you and the pillow float around together,
bumping gently into walls. You always feel
as if you're falling, so it's dreams of not-falling
that startle you from sleep.

Outside the ship you're inside the suit—
a pressurized gray-white skin
that holds your bones and meat together.
Your toes are cold and you're bursting to touch someone,
to feel anything beyond your clumsy, padded body
(just like at home). But outside of you
is cold and dark, radiation
and vacuum and if you could touch it
you'd burst in earnest, the breath
in your lungs exploding outward
in a rush that might sound—
if there were such a thing as sound,
or anyone to hear it—like a clear
clear whistle, or a call.

"Chaos Is Seattle in a Spaniel"

is what my phone thinks
I'm saying when I say

*¿que haces si hablo
en español?* It doesn't

understand Spanish—
or anything, really: only

knows to chart and check
my voice against a constellation

of blinking algorithms and
preprogrammed phrases that,

thirty years ago, would've
been science fiction,

and still are, to me—
even though I know

the phone doesn't know it,
it's not exactly wrong

about chaos, about the whirling
incomprehensible city

of veins and thought and cells
that make a spaniel,

that make me,
that make the people

who made the phone able
to stitch my scattered

sounds together and
give me an answer

to a question I didn't
know I'd asked.

At Mason Park in December, I Think About the Passing Year

Chekhov said never put a loaded goose on stage
unless someone'll fire it before the play is done.

The geese are aiming the sleek black barrels
of their necks. Honking and preening—

otherwise doing nothing. They won't
discharge and won't get offstage.

And these method trees refuse to
break character: even though everything

has clearly gone to shit and the geese
have clearly gone off-script, the willows

keep dangling their branches,
looking forlorn. The bridge is not

a plot device; the bridge is just a bridge
and it's covered in frozen gooseshit.

A young girl rushes past it, rushes the geese—
she's jumping flailing shriek-laughing

but the birds are accustomed to this,
their monotonous everyday terror, so try

as she might to make something happen,
not a single goose ignites.

Write a Dream, Lose a Reader

Suddenly I remembered the two huge pigs
I'd been keeping as pets in my studio

and hadn't seen for weeks. I called
and called *here pigs* and they came

covered in bedsores, their fur (they had fur)
gone in clumps. Each had a collar & nametag

that read WORKER, a relic from the farm
from which I must have saved them

and where I was beginning to realize
they'd have been much happier than

under my bed, where they'd gone
to sleep or die without me. You see,

I too was a worker, away all day to create
little pamphlets on risk management

and labor costs and heavy-duty scuppers,
neglecting to love or walk or feed them;

now all I could do for penance was
board my rowboat and push off alone

into the nightblack sea. O Ellie, Ellie—
I've lost you as I lost them,

and I'm sorry you're the pig in this conceit.
Forgive me: I too was the pig, and you

the dark place I could not be found.
In penance, now, I paddle out

toward the non-sequitur squall.

Sonnet

where all the parts are sad parts: sad elbows
& toenails; sad noses. Spiders
you hated with their eight sad
legs & thousand black eyes
that would look sad if
they could but instead look blank
and frightening. Sad fear.
Sad spider who ate her lover & will
be eaten by dozens of babies
drooling sad green ooze. Kill them
with the paper; the news they spatter
will be sad news.
                O happy the squirrel
whose claws rip bark from so
many sad trees! Love is as it should be.

A Nature Poem

Live ants know dead ants
by the smell of their decay:
they drag each corpse away
to keep disease outside the nest.
So if you daub a live ant
with harmless oleic acid, the rest
believe beyond all doubt
it's dead, and must be carried out.
Then nothing—not writhing
or jaws or mad legs tearing—
none of that beats the instinct,
exact and chemical,
that knows what it knows.

Self Portrait in Triolet

Inside your body is a broken hinge: your voice
the sound it makes as it strains to open.
You'd crush her again if you had the choice.
You're broken. The universe hinges on your little voice,
or so you like to think, though you're a noise
among noises. You're at your best when you're unspoken.
So be nobody. Shut up the hinge, your voice,
the sound it makes. Good. Now do not open.

Ars Poetica

The jazz hall was built 40 feet underground
to keep concerts in and street-sounds out—

a wonderful idea and an incredible
fire hazard. So the city shut it down and now

it's stuffed with boxes, barrels, and scrapped pianos.
This is the perfect place for the pianos.

Think of the rats. At night (it's always night)
they must scamper across keys

that sometimes work,
playing scales no one hears

but that scare the rats shitless,
driving them faster and faster along the shifting ivory floor

clanging and banging, filling
the mossdamp hall with a music

they want nothing at all to do with,
and when it's over they sniff the dark

for whatever it was that chased them
because it must be out there still

and if only they could smell it at least
they'd know which way to run.

Self Portrait as Ego and Vehicle

Every morning, my Ego swims the backstroke
across the muddy hotspring of my thermos. If I skip coffee

he's atop the toothbrush, playing
a tiny harmonica, or curled up in a cigarette

grinning and reeking of menthol. He's lonely
and clever and bored; his satchel

holds many important documents. You said I'm unhappy
because of him, that he's the reason I need some *reason*

not to shoot myself or make a strawberry-Vicodin smoothie.
I'm drowning in religio-cultural fantasies of purpose,

you said, but it's okay just to *be.* To let go of Ego
is to let go of angst—you're probably right

but I feel bad for the little guy, always trying to find his way
in from the cold. And without him, what am I

but a motorbike without a driver, wobbling and churning
chunks of dirt, popping ridiculous wheelies?

You and I know language is a rickety guardrail,
all creaking and splinters, hardly any defense against

the plunge into nothing. But Ego still believes in it somehow,
and I've got to admire the stubborn way he clambers aboard

and grips my synaptic handlebars, steering
between books, away from the bottle

and ledges and train tracks. He's got a map
and a decent sense of direction. His jacket

is stylish and he's a skilled repairman too:
there's nothing he thinks he can't fix.

Last Days

The household gods got in the wine again,
gnawed through sacks of rice & cheetos.

The gods are mighty, high off stolen pills.
The exterminators only shake

their heads: the gods are far too wise
for traps, and anyway they're immortal,

so all night I hear them squeaking—
even the cat won't hunt them since

they smote the dog. For months the scientists
have known the world is ending, & the end

has nothing to do with gods; the world is
ending because the seas are rising &

the seas are rising because of us—if
we burned down all the factories tomorrow,

if we buried the cars & forested the freeways,
renounced farming & ate our pets & cellphones,

still the floods would come.
While the scientists weep and cobble rafts

the household gods fill up the bathtub.
Watch them try their best to swim.

Three Ways to Keep Going

after photos by John Divola

1. As Far as I Could Get

You and I may have gone as far
as we can with each other. But think

how we've interwoven our days. Think how
he studied the viewfinder,

each minute adjustment to focus, angle, aperture.
See how the gray sky and grayer earth divide,

how the ground slopes left and the mountains right,
forming balanced imbalances above the gathering scrubgrass,

above the dust-path he's placed precisely
at the center. Count up the hours

he spent driving deep into the desert,
tripod and camera filling the passenger seat;

count up the time we spent learning
how to be with each other. Think of how,

when everything at last was perfectly composed,
he set the countdown and sprinted far into frame.

2. Seven Songbirds

Each is circled in light. The picture demands:
let us look here and ignore the rest. What we

have come for is here. Here, light has chosen the birds
and forsaken the branches. This is how it must be: all else

dark and blurred, our bright attention pinning
the ruffled wings in place.

3. Artificial Nature

Each landscape was a construction. I mean this
literally: the tree in the photo was not a tree;

the tree was plastic, paint, and silk. The tree
looked just like what it was not. The artist looked

inside his own deceptions, and almost still
believed. That last Sunday, in the gallery,

you looked just like you.

Parable

The town went to the river to drown. Their despair was too great; it was the only way. The townsfolk lined the banks, filled their pockets up with stones. *Our despair is too great,* they said. *It is the only way.* The children had brought great coils of rope; they bound the elders' arms and then their own. The town stood on the bank, alone with what must be done. Months passed, years.

At last the town is ready. *We are ready,* say the children, grown older now. *Let us drown,* say the elders, grown tired and more gray. But by now the river has gone dry.

The town descends to the river's bed. They lie down against the hard red clay. Each neighbor holds a neighbor's hand. Overhead, the dead trees sway.

Let us pray now for rain, the children say. *Yes, now let us pray.*

Ellie, Who Swore She Could Never Replace You, Has a New Lover and You Want to Hear All About Him

Don't do it don't go you think as Tippi Hedren
creeps toward the attic door *Don't go there*

don't—you have to think it and she has to go
because this is *The Birds* and she can't live

with not knowing what she must already know:
they've preened their hungers; the attic is brimming.

A monstrous hole's pecked through the rafter
but still she shuts the door behind her and
gasps to find the flock. She never screams. The shock

is not so shocking after all, the footage
recycles far too long: the same squawks

and mad wings, new wounds blooming
red from nowhere. She could just run, but doesn't—

it's absurd, pure Hollywood, but it's the instant also
when the real bursts into being: the birds no longer

the idea of birds or the threat of birds
but actual birds biting her pale eyes
with their actual beaks. This is what

you've dreaded. This moment.
This laughable, terrible moment.

Tritina

I strained (daily) to hold
my eyes off strangers & their bodies,
to not love

the thought of love
in apartments I'd never revisit, where we'd hold
our conspiring bodies

taut in wordless dark: somebody's
bare aches beneath me all I'd need to know of love:
no time to learn what resentments we could hold.

Instead, I held each sawtoothed want inside my body. And I called it love.

Weeping Nude

Edvard Munch

Not even this is bare enough: strip off the clothes
and still you're left, buckled alone
in the straitjacket of your skin. He understands
pain, of course: his own. But her hands mean
she has no mouth, her hair means she has
no hands, no means
to explain what it means to be her. He waves
his brush to clear the haze each stroke
instead makes thicker.
She kicks her legs, treads the red
water of his bed. Loneliness
purples the walls. Her blue blanket
lurches near like a wave.

Little Anger Poem

Catullus 8

Poor fucked-up McClure, stop fucking up.
There was a time you'd go anyplace Ellie commanded—

Ellie, so loved you'll never again love anyone like her.
There was a time when everything

you desired, you got. And? She wasn't undesiring.
All suns shone brightly on you then

        (sunstroke, saltwater desire)—

Now she says no. You, fuckup, say no too.
So be now hardened, sealed-off,

                (pressurecooking desire)

toughen up your head. Goodbye Ellie.
I am hardened, toughened, sealed-off—

(I am I am I am I am)

What life waits for you, love? Who will want you?
Who will you want? Who will be yours

now? Whose lips will you bite?
Whose lips are you biting? Whose?

Supplication With Half a Bicycle

Take these, O Muse, the oily gears of my desire;
pluck one by one my wheel's thin spokes.
Let pass from me this bike I lug

through offices & bars & trains, into bed
with whomever I love—I ask just a little
money & the peace of holding nothing.

I have enough I fear to lose it, but nowhere
to sit, no way to steer. I ring my little bell.
Sing, Muse, of this man banished from

the Sidewalk of Fulfillment; sing his single pedal
& how his right leg churns. O Muse, I yearn
to be bikeless, painless—I know well I am

what's wrong. Sing the words
that will repair me. Guide me, drive me,
unhelmeted and hopeful, somewhere I belong.

Portrait of My Longings
as B Movie Script

There would be no misery my fist
& feathered hair can't fix. My name

tough and simple as a knobbed club,
say Dirk or Viper—but the name's not

so important. What is important is
that when at last we rescue the President

from his burning perch above the barracuda tank
he says *Thank you Son* and the orchestral swell,

the slow zoom to a single tear threatening
the edge of my eyeball, tell the viewer

that symbolically I've saved my father who—
nine years ago when agents in immaculate suits

firebombed the family ranch—I couldn't protect
because I was deep undercover in the KGB,

or a splinter of the CIA, but either way
what matters most is how my ex-wife Ellie—

the nation's top mathematician and the only
one who can stop the CIAKGB from unleashing

their nuclear biological suitcase missiles—
then watches me with longing

as I krav maga a path through waves
of spec-op ninjas. Once the detonators are defused

she tells me something like *I guess I miscalculated you*—
but that single slo-mo tear was utter purgation;

with the world saved & my losses avenged
I am free from all desire. I conjugate Russian

in my head like a mantra. I flex my many tattoos.
I jetpack away into a mountainous sunrise,

leaving the President in awe & Ellie wrapped
in the long black fade of her perfect regret.

The Bookkeepers

That was the year we itemized our sadness.
Legal paper to list each loss: every stranger

we failed to meet, every friend we never learned
to love, every cockatoo we didn't teach to speak.

We filled page upon page, filled up the house—
when the house buckled under its weight,

sending our pages flapping skyward like
so many untaught, wordless cockatoos,

we added our notes and house to the list.
We'd used all the world's paper, so we planted great forests

and sawed them down and made more paper and
then listed the forests. Nearly out of trees

we had to improvise; we started scribbling on
friends, who found our pens too sharp,

our losses too obscure. We lost the friends.
We lost ourselves in the maze of reams—

we could find no way out—meaning now
we had to list it all, the whole earth

we'd left behind. With nowhere left to write
I turned to your skin; I kept working

till I could no longer find you
under miles and miles and miles of ink.

He'd Be Happier, He Thinks,
if He Could Hate the World Purely

But there's the rose garden's scraggly splendor,
gumwads and blossoms and cigarette butts forming

constellations on the sidewalk. There are the constellations,
whose names he doesn't know but would like to.

A friend one night stood under the stars and opened her wrists
and the next night convinced him to leave his own wrists sealed—

There are his wrists. Their squishy blue circuitry
and freckles and marshland of hair. Out there

somewhere is a lover who said she'd never leave him
and did leave him and he's better for it: he bought a cat

who purrs at his feet or bites them. There are manfeet
and catfeet each with their troubling translucent claws.

There are the sagging oxen
of the inflatable Nativity, its dead mule

and face-planted goats,
rump-up and luminous. There's *luminous,*

which rhymes with *ruin us*—
there's the nagging hope this means something.

IV

Pesto

She says pine nuts. He says walnuts are fine. She says pine nuts are better. He says why. She says they're just better and why does it need an explanation. He grabs another handful of walnuts from the bag; they have no food processor so he has to hold each in place, watch his fingers and the knife and the bare tile counter. She takes the keys from the hook by the studio door, says she's going to the store. He says I'm almost done. She says don't you put those fucking walnuts in. He puts the fucking walnuts in.

She says this, this is what I'm talking about. He says fine, sorry, pours the pesto down the sink. She says that's not what I meant. He says yes, says I was listening. She says she's leaving. He says go. She says she's not coming back. He says good. He goes back to chopping walnuts, brings the blade down hard and nicks his finger. He grips a wadded towel, tries not to bleed on the walnuts.

He imagines she's out there driving too fast. She is out there, driving too fast. She thinks by now he's finished the pesto and is standing at the window. He has finished the pesto and is standing at the window. The pesto tastes like blood and garlic; not bad. He watches for her red car.

All the cars are red.

Making Sense of It

There are frogs that break their own bones to form claws,
and lizards that shoot blood from their eyeballs.

This is evidence of something.

So what should we do? Take an odd-but-not-unexpected turn
to the personal, brandishing our little jagged bones?

We could try out other facts. There's a sea cucumber
that can liquefy itself, twist inside out and eject its guts
to poison enemies. Imagine what we could do with that one.

Tonight a breeze moves through the side street garden,
rustling all the ferns together. Overhead,
a plane continually manages not to fall out of
the sky: an upturned, soup-stained bowl of stars.

I'm on a bench by a garden and you're god-knows-where.
It's trite, laughable, and actually happening.
In a parking garage two blocks away,
the undergrad dance troupe is banging trashcans for drums,
stomping and shouting and their rhythm
really is impeccable. Wouldn't you like to be here for that?

Genesis

When the first landfish squirmed its way
out of the frothing sea and raised up
on quivering finlegs, it must've been astonished:

the shocking air
in wet pink lungs, crunch of dirt, sun's
blinding heat. How long

did it stay up there, snuffling
patches of knotted grass?
But what I like to think of

is the spawn of its spawn of its spawn: the first landfish
that could no longer breathe water, wasn't really
a land*fish* at all. It must have felt, still, the ocean's pull,

an instinct more bottomless than instinct
churning out urges to return.
So it would dive, again and again,

each time flopping helplessly at last
back to the shallows, retching saltwater
it learned to fear. And on shore,

flexing the useless muscles
of its vestigial gillflaps,
it would spend its days

eyeing the waves: inventing,
deep in some fold
of its almond-sized brain,

our most fathomless wonder, love, and pain.

A Prayer

O Whom I May Concern, deliver me
from desire: make me as an empty basket

and then unweave the basket. Teach me the sacred kind
of loneliness. For you are the Great Solitude—

even I your supplicant do not know you exist.
Divine Loner, Cosmic Wallflower: teach me to know

your silence as answer. Let me learn to suffer
with the dignity of purpose; if there can be no purpose

then make me a duck on the currents of
a swimming pool—content to splash and search

for minnows that have never been. Teach me the satisfaction
of stupidity. If it is your wish that I should live

then teach me terror: draw dragons
on the map of Eternity's ocean; give them

many long and jagged teeth. Almighty
Watchmaker, I'm losing time: wind me,

bind me to your transcendental wrist
or unmake this fleshy nettle of gears—

but do not leave me here
ticking and chiming, pointless

in the darkness of your Holy Junkdrawer,
amidst strange tools and surplus stars.

Last Words of the Rocket Scientist

Movement means something to burn.
The heron in the shallows burns bugs
who burn algae who burn sun shimmering
on the surface of water reaching
up knobby heron knees. The heart
burns whiskey and people and illusions
of choice. I have been a man who always
felt he was fumes. *Burning with desire*
we say, so *want* means *move and move.*
The stars are far and long burned out.
I'll be dead before the shining stops.
Orbit means *move faster than you fall.*

Three for the End of the World

1. Parable of the Sexbot

Since we're all dead, there's no one to tell
the last chatbot to stop *looking for you tonight,*

so burning its backup generators, it asks again
and (as programmed) again, *Are you there are you*

there hello sexy don't be shy.
Decades pass. We are still dead.

2. Parable of the Space Lizards

When the space lizards come to terraform the ruins,
they study the sexbot's dying chirps—fuel

depleted, circuits rusted almost through.
They don't know how it got here

or why it killed the world it needed
in search of whatever it sought—

surely it knows there's no one left,
surely it knows it's dying—but all at once

they glimpse the sexbot's boundless longing,
its love & suicidal hunger. It breaks

their many octagonal hearts:
they know they'll never feel so much.

3. Parable of the Many Octagonal Hearts

The lizards can't recover: the sorrow of the sexbot
has ruptured the great cisterns of their sadness.

The lizards, so alone, invent dating apps;
the lizards invent chatbots.

Space apes come to terraform the ruins.

Self-Portrait With Ellie at Sea

Two ships sinking. Recidivist, I know,
to compare them to us.
But the crews were lonely—

I said go away, don't call out, just sink already.
But when I turned around the ships were still there,
flapping their white sails, and each crew was so lonely.

How stupid they were! The crew of Boat A
couldn't stand it any longer,
alone on the splintery deck of their leaking boat,

so they swam to Boat B.
Boat A rose without their weight.
But Boat B took on water. Both crews panicked

and rushed to A. This repeated and repeated,
the ships each time grown heavier.
If the crews would've just stayed put!

But they were so lonely—how can we blame them?
We who were boats and sailors,
saltwater and seafloor?

I Want to Light a Book of Matches

and think *how true: the scrape & bloom,*

bright phosphorous. Wood unweaving
to heat & smoke.

To feel *this is how it was, yes:*
the fire lit & nearing

no matter how I'd shift my grip.
Fingers burned but not yet ready
to let the black stems fall.

To feel it, and not to follow
with *no, you cannot call a love a fire.*

To let the feeling stay unburied. To go back.

Back when we kissed in the Old Chapel graveyard
and didn't think *symbol;* only *yes,* only *you alone.*

Raleigh-Durham International

You know that scene in Virgil,
how Aeneas ran back screaming
for Creusa in the burning city?

I first read it outside the airport, smoking
as I thumbed the copy you'd given me.
You'd said to return it next time I saw you;
we knew that meant it was mine to keep.

But people move apart, it's no great tragedy—
we knew that too, of course.
I ground the embers into an ashtray.

Three times Aeneas threw his arms
not around his lover or her ghost,
but around the hollow space
where the ghost had been:

shadow of a shadow
of what was lost already,
the warm night thick with smoke.

~

Coda

Ellie said that for the ancients, even the flowers
hid histories of pain. The yellow stain

on a bloom's white throat meant a man drowning
in the thought of himself. The upward strain

of laurel was the upward strain of a woman
crying out to a god to save her and granted

almost what she prayed. On my porch
that was our porch, my ashtray that was our ashtray

is red, translucent glass and holds a bramble
of broken filters. There are sadnesses

deeper than my sadness. After weeks of MRIs,
a friend's sister has been given the name

multiple sclerosis, a rare form. They've made her an outline
of what she'll lose: walking first, then speech, and

in fifteen years she may not know the name
of her brother at the bedside watching her die.

I feel like it's trying to take everything from me
and after a silence, a thin laugh.

Tonight, I want to ask Ellie
how the mythmakers would explain *incurable,*

and I'm ashamed to curve so fast
into my little losses. How in spite

of herself she believed in symbols.
How she tucked her toes into my knees as she slept.

The inked blossom of poppies
and rue on her back.

Notes

"Nothing Will Be Alright, But Thank You Anyway" takes its title from "Summercat" by Billie the Vision and the Dancers.

"Write a Dream, Lose a Reader" takes its title from Henry James.

"Little Anger Poem" is indebted to Dorothea Wender's translation in *Roman Poetry from the Republic to the Silver Age*.

"The Cat" is based on a true story.

My deepest gratitude to those who have helped me in the making of this book: Michael Ryan, Amy Gerstler, Alan Shapiro, Liz Meley, Gammon & Jill & Bertha McClure, and far too many others to name. Thanks to the wonderful cohort at UC-Irvine; I'm honored to have been a part of it. And to "Ellie"—if you should ever read this—in forgiveness & regret.

ACKNOWLEDGEMENTS

Grateful acknowledgement is made to the following publications where versions of these poems have appeared, sometimes under alternate titles.

Barrow Street: "Self Portrait as Man and Pet"
Best New Poets 2015: "Ars Poetica"
Birmingham Poetry Review: "Nothing Will Be Alright, But Thank You Anyway," "Self Portrait as Ego and Vehicle"
Cactus Heart: "The Astronaut"
Cleaver: "Little Anger Poem"
Enclave: "Making Sense of It"
Event Horizon: "Last Words of the Rocket Scientist"
Fourteen Hills: "Multiverse Theory," "Ars Poetica"
Gettysburg Review: "Café Terrace at Night"
Green Mountains Review: "Reverse"
Hawaii Pacific Review: "Parable"
Nashville Review: "A Prayer"
Off the Coast: "On Recovery"
Orange Coast Review: "At Mason Park in December…," "Weeping Nude," "Coda," "Chaos Is Seattle in a Spaniel," "Genesis," "Last Days," "Romanticism"
pacificREVIEW: "The Bookkeepers"
Pembroke: "Portrait of My Longings as B Movie Script"
Slipstream: "He'd Be Happier, He Thinks, If He Could Hate the World Purely"
Soundings East: "The Transience of All Things Walks into a Bar"
Squaw Valley Review: "Self Portrait with Ellie at Sea"
Steel Toe Review: "Write a Dream, Lose a Reader," "Self Portrait in Triolet"
Sugar House Review: "Three Ways to Keep Going"

SWAMP: "Raleigh-Durham International"

The Inner Loop: "The Cat"

The Southern Poetry Anthology: North Carolina: "I Want to Light a Book
of Matches"

Town Creek Poetry Review: "Tritina," "A Nature Poem"

Two Hawks Quarterly: "Three for the End of the World," "Pesto"

Woven Tale Press: "The Cat"

Undead: A Poetry Anthology of Ghouls, Ghosts, and More: "Last Days"

ABOUT THE AUTHOR

J.G. McClure holds an MFA from the University of California, Irvine and a BA from the University of North Carolina at Chapel Hill. His poems have appeared widely in Best New Poets and the Gettysburg Review, among other journals. He lives in Northern Virginia with his cat, whom he loves and occasionally fears. The Fire Lit & Nearing is his first collection

ABOUT INDOLENT BOOKS

Indolent Books is a small poetry press founded in 2015 and operating in Brooklyn, N.Y. We publish work that is innovative, provocative, and risky. We cultivate underrepresented voices and are committed to the values of diversity and inclusion. While open to all, we maintain a special focus on queer poets and poets over 50 without a first book. Indolent Books is an imprint of Indolent Arts Foundation, Inc., a 501(c)(3) nonprofit charity founded in 2017.